WARTIME SPIES

CREATIVE EDUCATION • CREATIVE PAPERBACKS

COLD
WAR SPIES

MICHAEL E. GOODMAN

Published by Creative Education and Creative Paperbacks
P.O. Box 227, Mankato, Minnesota 56002
Creative Education and Creative Paperbacks are imprints of
The Creative Company
www.thecreativecompany.us

Design and production by Chelsey Luther
Art direction by Rita Marshall
Printed in Malaysia

Photographs by Corbis (Bettmann, Günter Bratke/dpa, CORBIS,
La Tercera/Reuters, NSA/Handout, Science Photo Library, Alex
Milan Tracy/Demotix), Dreamstime (VanderWolf Images), Flickr
(The Central Intelligence Agency), Getty Images (AFP, Adam Berry,
Ctsy. John Hallisey, Bob Gomel/Time Life Pictures, Keystone/
Hulton Archive, Keystone/Stringer, New York Daily News Archive,
Popperfoto), International Spy Museum (Permanent Collection),
Lost & Taken (Brant Wilson), TextureX.com (TextureX), Vector-
Templates.com

Library of Congress Cataloging-in-Publication Data
Goodman, Michael E.
Cold War spies / Michael E. Goodman.
p. cm. — (Wartime spies)
Summary: A historical account of espionage during the Cold War,
including famous spies such as Aldrich Ames, covert missions, and
technologies that influenced the course of the conflict.
Includes bibliographical references and index.
ISBN 978-1-60818-599-3 (hardcover)
ISBN 978-1-62832-204-0 (pbk)
1. Cold War—Juvenile literature. 2. Espionage—History—20th
century—Juvenile literature. I. Title.

D843.G643 2015
327.1209'045—dc23   2014037531

CCSS: RI.5.1, 2, 3, 5, 6, 8; RH.6-8.3, 4, 5, 6, 7, 8, 9

First Edition HC 9 8 7 6 5 4 3 2 1
First Edition PBK 9 8 7 6 5 4 3 2 1

CONTENTS

AIRBORNE SPY

On May 1, 1960, Francis Gary Powers, an American pilot flying for the Central *Intelligence* Agency (CIA), took off from Pakistan in an ultra-modern, high-powered spy plane known as the U-2. He planned to fly over the Soviet Union at an altitude of more than 70,000 feet (21,336 m) to take photographs of new Soviet missile sites before landing safely in Norway. Suddenly, in mid-flight, a missile exploded near the aircraft, and the U-2 tumbled out of control. Powers had been trained to do two things if his top-secret plane was compromised: first, inject himself with poison, and then hit a switch to blow up the plane. As the aircraft spun, he was unable to do either. Instead, he was ejected from the plane and parachuted to the ground, where he was quickly captured. Within days, Soviet premier (government leader) Nikita Khrushchev publicly condemned the United States for heating up the Cold War with such an act of deception.

DIVIDED *by an* IRON CURTAIN

WORLD WAR II (1939–45) officially ended in Europe in May 1945. But a new and different type of conflict was just beginning. In the last years of the war, the army of the Soviet Union had pushed the Germans and their allies out of Eastern Europe. Although the Soviets were liberating countries such as Poland, Hungary, Czechoslovakia, and Yugoslavia, they had other motives. They wanted to control those countries politically and establish a buffer zone to keep their country safe from future attacks across its western borders. They also wanted to impose their political philosophy, known as *communism*, on them.

Though 1.8 million strong in 1939, the Soviets' Red Army was ill-prepared to face Nazi Germany.

Major Western nations—such as the U.S., Great Britain, and France—were nervous about such developments and believed they had to do something to limit Soviet territorial expansion and the spread of communism. The Soviets had been allies of the Western powers during much of World War II, as all were common enemies of the Germans. The relationship was not necessarily based on mutual trust, though. As the Soviets continued staking claims throughout Eastern Europe, British prime minister Winston Churchill described their activities as being like drawing an "iron curtain" or building an "iron fence." In a March 5, 1946, speech, Churchill said, "From Stettin in the Baltic [in Poland] to Trieste in the Adriatic [in Albania], an iron curtain has descended across the continent." Churchill and other Western leaders saw the Iron Curtain as an invisible but very real political barrier separating countries that favored *capitalism* and *democracy* from those that believed in communism.

Starting in 1946, a war was waged across the Iron Curtain for more than 40 years. For the most part, this war was fought not with tanks, fighter planes, warships, or bombs. Instead, the Cold War featured build-ups of destructive weapons by both sides, threatening standoffs, and new and inventive methods of spying on each other.

COVERT OPS
FLOATING SPIES

During the 1950s, the U.S. tried using unmanned balloons to spy on the Soviet Union. As part of Operation Moby Dick, balloons with cameras attached were launched from Scotland, Norway, Germany, and Turkey. The plan was to have them float from west to east across the Soviet Union, taking pictures until they reached the Pacific Ocean, where they would be picked up by American navy vessels. Many balloons were lost, and at least one camera was recovered by the Russians. In the 1950s, many people reported seeing unidentified flying objects (UFOs) in the sky that they thought came from other planets. Some of these may have been American balloons.

CHAPTER ONE

SPY VS. SPY

ON APRIL 12, 1945, U.S. president Franklin D. Roosevelt died of a massive stroke, and vice president Harry S. Truman was sworn in as his successor. Twelve days later, Truman was given his first briefing on the Manhattan Project—the program to create the atomic bomb. Until he became president, Truman had been told nothing about the top-secret project. Amazingly, Russian leader Joseph Stalin already knew all about America's secret weapons program. The Soviet Union had many spies in the U.S. before 1945, including some scientists working on the Manhattan Project itself, such as German-born physicist Klaus Fuchs. Like many of the other spies, Fuchs was a devoted communist and was happy to help the Soviets learn how to create their own atomic weapons and keep up with the U.S.

The *infiltration* of the Manhattan Project occurred during World War II, but it was a forewarning of the conflict to come. Some of the most important "soldiers" during the Cold War were *agents*, *moles*, *double agents*, and *defectors*—all working against each other to discover or protect secrets. Most key events in the Cold War featured "spy vs. spy" confrontations.

9.0 SEC.
N

⊢———⊣ 100 METERS

The U.S. had established its first professional intelligence network during World War II, known as the Office of Strategic Services (OSS). After the war, President Truman disbanded the OSS. However, he was convinced by 1947 that a full-time spy organization—to be named the Central Intelligence Agency—was needed, even in peacetime, to deal with potential communist threats. The CIA was charged with gathering and analyzing intelligence and coordinating covert (undercover, or hidden) operations designed to hinder communism and promote U.S. interests outside the country. Truman also agreed to expand the efforts of the Federal Bureau of Investigation (FBI) to handle counterespionage within the country—uncovering spy operations and capturing spies.

The FBI began working overtime on counterintelligence after the Soviet Union tested its first atomic bomb in 1949. There was a strong belief that the Russians must have had "inside" help learning atomic secrets, and the FBI was determined to ferret out Soviet spies who might have worked inside the Manhattan Project. One key method involved restudying Russian cables, or telegrams, intercepted during World War II. The messages, obtained as part of a top-secret U.S. military intelligence program called the Venona Project, provided clues to the identities of several possible spies. Fuchs became

a suspect and was arrested in late 1949. Under intense questioning, Fuchs confessed and implicated several others who

may have passed along sensitive nuclear information to the Russians.

The unassuming Fuchs began his atomic research while in Britain and was sent to the U.S. in 1943.

Eventually, the evidence led to a New York couple named Julius and Ethel Rosenberg. The Rosenbergs were convicted of treason in 1951 and were executed two years later. They would be the only Americans executed as spies by the U.S. during the Cold War. On the other side, numerous Russian operatives, or secret agents, caught spying against their country were put to death. How did the Soviets discover that some of their operatives were double agents for the

DANGLING THE TRUTH

A new type of spy was at work in the Cold War. Called a "dangle" in English or a *podstava* in Russian, they offered to change sides and become double agents but really stayed loyal to their original country. Once these "dangled" spies earned the trust of their new bosses, they could report back enemy secrets they learned or provide **disinformation** to mislead the enemy. Markus Wolf, the head of the East German intelligence agency known as Stasi, placed a number of dangles inside CIA groups working in his country. As a result, American intelligence reports about East Germany were often incorrect.

Remnants of equipment and furnishings from Stasi headquarters are preserved in a Berlin museum.

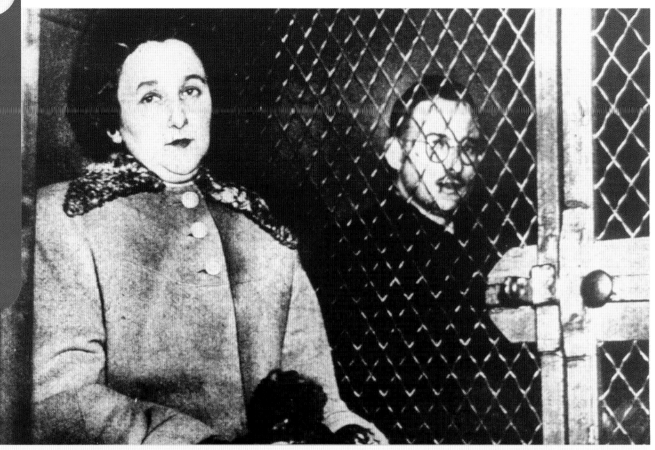

The Rosenbergs obtained atomic secrets from Ethel's brother, who worked at Manhattan Project labs.

West? In several cases, that information was provided by American or British intelligence officers who were working undercover for the Russians.

This may seem a little complicated, but remember the Cold War was a time of "spy vs. spy." Each side spent a great deal of time and money building large intelligence networks; bribing or persuading intelligence operatives for the other side to switch allegiance and become double agents; and designing new methods, tools, and gadgets both for spying and for countering spies.

Most of the Cold War spies, particularly those who turned against their own countries, did so for one of two reasons: (1) they believed in the ideals of one side, or (2) they were paid well. For example, Fuchs and the Rosenbergs believed strongly in communism, and that was their main motivation for revealing American secrets to the Soviet Union. On the other hand, several notorious American turncoats, such as naval officer John Walker, longtime FBI agent Robert Hanssen, and veteran CIA operative Aldrich Ames, agreed to spy in return for large cash payments from the Soviets.

One of the most important Russians to spy for the West, Oleg Penkovsky, a colonel in the Soviets' military intelligence organization GRU, switched sides for both ideological and financial reasons. Penkovsky had become disillusioned with the Soviet system and what he felt were Soviet threats to peace in the world. In December 1960, he offered his services to the British and Americans and agreed to photograph hundreds of secret Soviet documents with a miniature camera. Penkovsky also negotiated a high salary for his spy work.

Over the next year and a half, Penkovsky passed along briefcases filled with documents and rolls of film hidden inside boxes of candy or cigarette packages to British and American agents. The Russian mole provided secret information that helped diffuse one of the most threatening situations during the Cold War, the Cuban Missile Crisis. In October 1962, American spy planes detected Soviet missiles on the ground in Cuba, where Fidel Castro had set up a communist government only 90 miles (145 km) off the coast of Florida. U.S. president John F.

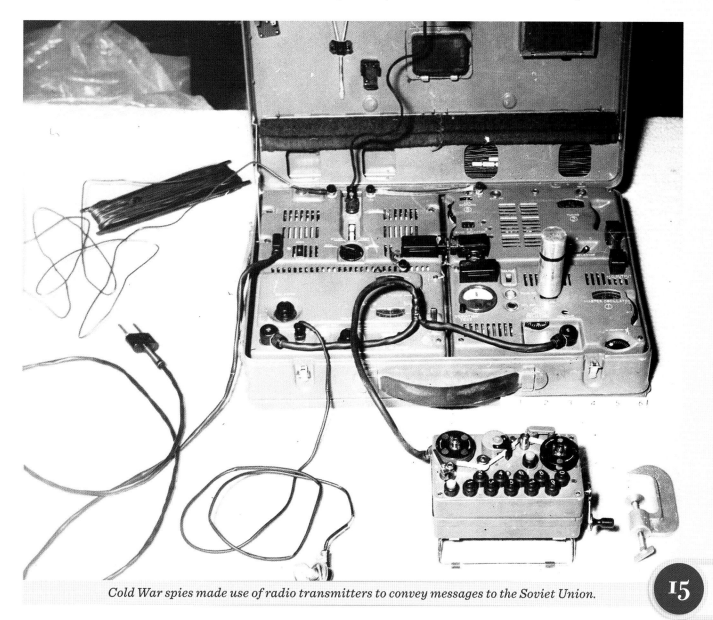

Cold War spies made use of radio transmitters to convey messages to the Soviet Union.

Kennedy confronted Soviet premier Nikita Khrushchev about the missiles and demanded that they be removed. People around the world held their breath in fear that the two superpowers might use nuclear weapons against each other, but Kennedy stood firm. His strong stance was bolstered in part by Penkovsky's assurances that the Russians did not yet have the capability to launch missiles accurately from Cuba. In the end, Khrushchev backed down. Meanwhile, the Russians suspected that Penkovsky might have been a source of American intelligence about their missiles. He was arrested a few days after the Cuban crisis ended and executed in May 1963. Several years later, a book entitled *The Spy Who Saved the World* was written about Penkovsky.

A few months before Penkovsky was executed in Moscow, another famous double agent arrived in the Soviet capital seeking *asylum*. The turncoat spy was Kim Philby, who had been a leader of Britain's MI6 (similar to the CIA) and at one time was in line to become its director. In the 1930s, Philby had attended Cambridge University, where he became close friends with four other young men who all believed in communism. All five were recruited by the Soviet security and intelligence service (later named the KGB) and willingly joined. After college, they all got important jobs in British intelligence agencies or the Foreign Office, which gave them access to secret information that they provided to the Soviet Union during and after World War II. Because of his MI6 position, Philby learned in 1951 that two of his classmates, Donald Maclean and Guy Burgess, were suspected of treason. He warned them, and both escaped to the Soviet Union.

After that, Philby was also closely watched to see if he might be a Soviet mole. He was forced to resign from MI6 but then was reinstated with the support of British prime minister Harold MacMillan, who mistakenly called Philby an "upstanding citizen" and "hero." After several defectors from Russia later identified Philby as a mole, he fled to Moscow in January 1963 and became a Soviet citizen. British intelligence leaders were ashamed to discover that one of their stars had been so disloyal, but Philby was just one among many spies who switched sides during the Cold War.

At a 1955 press conference, Philby brazenly denied being the "Third Man" to Burgess and Maclean.

CHAPTER TWO

GO, GO, GADGET

FOR HUNDREDS OF YEARS, spying was done by human operatives using their own quick thinking, tricks and deceptions, and simple tools. In spy talk, this was called HUMINT, or human intelligence. Then new technical tools were invented—from miniaturized cameras to devices used for secretive listening, broadcasting, and recording. These tools made it easier for spies to observe events, copy documents the enemy wanted to keep hidden, send coded messages, or eavesdrop on private conversations. When spies used these tools, they were combining HUMINT with TECHINT, or technical intelligence.

By the Cold War years, even more advanced tools were available—from ultrasonic spy planes equipped with high-power cameras to spy satellites to sophisticated message-interception equipment. Such tools enabled spy agencies to carry out new types of espionage called IMINT (image intelligence), SIGINT (signals intelligence), or COMINT (communications intelligence). Two of the most significant events during the Cold War years involved inventions used for spying from the sky. Both events increased tensions between the two sides in the conflict.

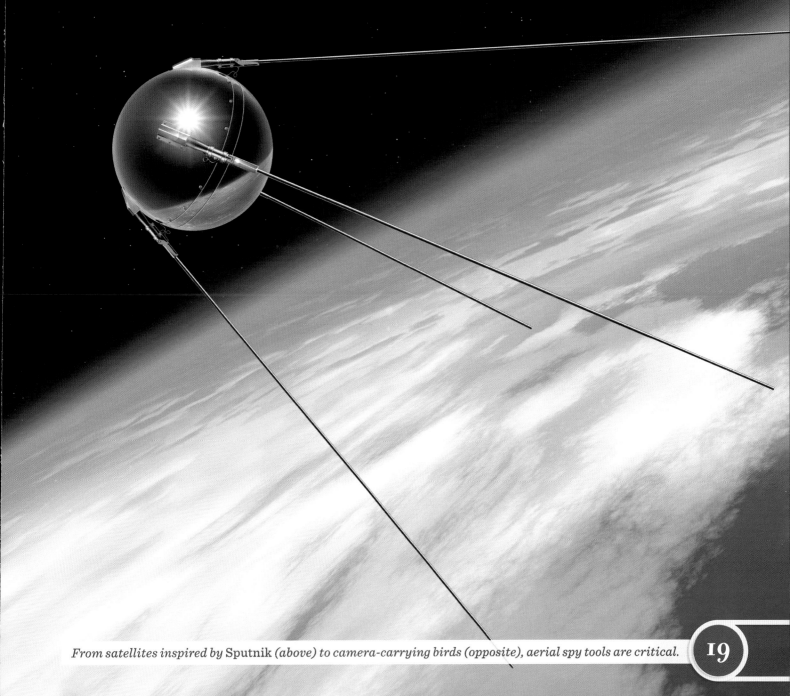

From satellites inspired by Sputnik (above) to camera-carrying birds (opposite), aerial spy tools are critical.

The first event was announced to American readers in huge capital letters across the front page of the *New York Times* on October 5, 1957: "SOVIET FIRES EARTH SATELLITE INTO SPACE; IT IS CIRCLING THE GLOBE AT 18,000 MPH; SPHERE TRACKED IN 4 CROSSINGS OVER U.S." The previous day, the Soviets had launched the world's first man-made satellite, *Sputnik*, a Russian word meaning "traveling companion (of Earth)." *Sputnik* was about the size of a basketball, weighed 183 pounds (83 kg), and took 98 minutes to circle the globe. The Soviets planned to use *Sputnik* to help them spy on other countries. They probably also saw their new tool as a way to scare the West—and it worked. American scientists, politicians, and other citizens immediately began worrying that rockets that could launch a satellite such as *Sputnik* might also be able to send nuclear weapons toward the U.S. The Americans were also embarrassed that the Russians were taking the lead in space technology.

Two months later, they were even more embarrassed when the U.S. attempted to launch its own satellite, known as Vanguard, and the rocket carrying the satellite exploded on the launch pad. In March 1958, the *Vanguard I* satellite was finally launched into Earth orbit. It carried two radios and a temperature sensor and was the first orbiting vehicle to be powered by solar energy. The radio signals it bounced off Earth proved that our planet was slightly elliptical in shape rather than perfectly round. That satellite is still circling Earth today.

The U.S. and Soviet Union now found themselves in a new type of competition—a "space race." Over the next 20 years, each side would spend billions of dollars sending people into space or designing new types of aerial weapons and spy satellites. One U.S. satellite program that played an important role in Cold War spying was called Corona. The first Corona satellite was launched in August 1960 and was used for

The December 1957 explosion of the two-stage rocket carrying Vanguard was a temporary setback.

A GARBAGE BAG WORTH MILLIONS

Senior FBI agent Robert Hanssen spied for the Soviet Union for more than 20 years before he was finally caught in 2001. He avoided capture for so long because he was very careful. Even his Russian *handler* did not know his real name or what he looked like. Hanssen usually left secret documents or computer files for the Russians in garbage bags at Washington-area *dead drops*. He was finally caught when the FBI offered a former KGB agent millions of dollars for evidence that could identify the mole working inside the Bureau. The Russian provided a garbage bag that had Hanssen's fingerprints on it and a recording of his voice, which helped prove his guilt.

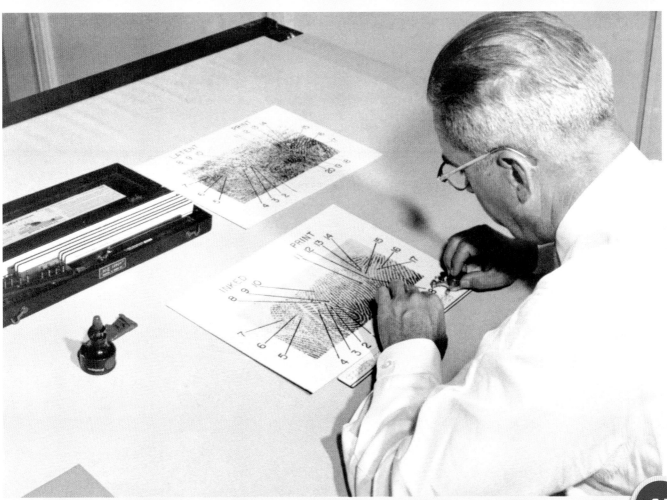

Fingerprinting experts at the FBI use physical evidence to identify criminals such as Hanssen.

reconnaissance purposes. It took photographs of the Iron Curtain countries from more than 100 miles (161 km) above the earth. Then the film was moved into a special reentry capsule that would fall to Earth on a parachute and be collected. Later, each side developed spy satellites that could transmit pictures directly back to Earth.

The second major spy-in-the-sky event occurred on May 1, 1960, when CIA pilot Francis Gary Powers's U-2 spy plane was shot down by Russian missiles. During the flight (one of many that he made over Russia), Powers had been taking pictures of Soviet military installations with special high-altitude cameras. When he was captured on the ground, Powers was carrying papers that identified him as a CIA operative. He also admitted under questioning that he was a spy. CIA leaders did not realize at first what had happened to Powers. They believed he had killed himself and destroyed the plane as he had been trained to do. When Premier Khrushchev accused the U.S. of high-altitude spying, American leaders insisted that the plane was simply checking weather conditions when it crashed. Then Khrushchev revealed photographs of Powers in Soviet custody and copies of the aerial photos he had been taking. Once again, the U.S. looked incompetent to the rest of the world. Powers was tried and imprisoned. In 1962, he and another prisoner were exchanged for a Russian spy named Rudolf Abel and returned to the U.S.

Not all Cold War technology was designed for highflying spying. One of the most surprising tools was a bug (a secretive listening device) discovered in the American *embassy* in Moscow in May 1952. The listening device was hidden inside a large replica of the Great Seal of the United States that had been presented to the U.S. ambassador in 1946 as a gift from Soviet children. The Russians used the bug to eavesdrop on meetings that took place in the embassy for more than six years. It was finally discovered during a careful sweep for listening devices. The U.S. did not make its discovery public until 1960, however, waiting until the United Nations (UN) Security Council was meeting at the Soviets' insistence to discuss the U-2 incident. Then America's UN ambassador, Henry Cabot Lodge Jr., displayed the bug to show that

As Ambassador Lodge pointed out, the bug in the Great Seal had been implanted beneath the eagle's beak.

A German-invented camera worn as a wristwatch became a popular Cold War spy accessory.

the Soviet Union was equally guilty of conducting covert operations.

Technology experts during the Cold War also found ingenious ways to help human agents hide cameras, microphones, and recording devices for spying. One such tool used by spies in East Germany was a tiny reel-to-reel tape recorder that was no bigger than a deck of cards but could hold many minutes of conversation picked up by a microphone hidden inside a wristwatch. The spy would conceal the cord connecting the watch and tape recorder under a jacket sleeve. In Russia, a company designed a shoe with a hollow heel in which a tiny camera could be stored. Another Russian company designed a tie capable of hiding a small camera, with its lens opening through a special tie tack. The agent could substitute a real tie tack when not taking pictures. There were

also cameras hidden in the handles of canes or inside pens and briefcases. The CIA even created a tiny spying device that looked and acted like a dragonfly. The technical name for this type of tool was "micro unmanned aerial vehicle," or micro-UAV. It could flutter inside a room and take pictures or record sound.

A number of clever but simple tools were used as ways for spies to conceal evidence they wanted to convey to their handlers. A hollowed-out spike provided an ideal place to hide film or rolled-up documents. The spike could then be pushed into the ground at a dead drop, where handlers would retrieve it. A microdot camera was another useful spy tool. Agents would use the camera to photograph documents. They could then shrink the developed images to the size of tiny dots, which could be hidden in the text of an innocent-looking letter, sometimes as punctuation marks. The microdots could be read using a special magnifying viewer. For Cold War spies, inventive tools such as these were vital for staying ahead of the competition.

While micro-UAVs (bottom) and microdot cameras (middle) collected intel on their own, sometimes a drill was needed to implant audio devices (top).

CHAPTER THREE
WOMEN KEEP INFORMED

AS THEY HAD DURING World War II, women took on major intelligence roles in the Cold War. Women operatives, *cryptanalysts*, and counterespionage experts stepped forward in this new conflict. We don't know full details about many of these remarkable women because they chose to work in the shadows, and few wrote about their exploits. Some do stand out, however, and helped to influence espionage between 1945 and the early 1990s.

A good example was Elizabeth Swantek, who worked for the Army Signal Corps during World War II, analyzing enemy communications. After the war, she went to college, where she majored in political science and languages and became fluent in Russian. In 1951, she joined the CIA and was sent to southern Germany to train several volunteers, all former Soviet citizens living in Western Europe, to infiltrate their former country. The volunteers were expected to establish new, hidden lives in the Soviet Union and wait to be contacted to carry out spy missions. Then they would hopefully be brought safely out of the country.

The intensive training lasted six months. Swantek taught the trainees spy *tradecraft*, including how to parachute from a plane, how

Spies and military intelligence officers were trained to evade capture (above) and decode messages (opposite). 27

to survive in the wild, how to establish a new identity, and how to use a wireless radio to transmit messages. Then she made sure that their clothing, appearance, and papers were in order and wouldn't give them away as spies. Most of the trainees successfully avoided capture and established their new lives in Russia. They braved danger to send radio messages back to their handlers. The messages provided assurances that the Soviets were not planning an all-out attack on Europe, which some Western military experts feared at the time.

Later, Swantek took on several other important CIA assignments, using a variety of *covers*. "During my career, I wore many faces," she told an interviewer after she retired from the CIA. "I was a tour director, a buyer, someone's girlfriend, a photographer, an art collector, and even a young teenage boy."

Another female intelligence leader, Juanita Moody, was an unsung hero of the Cuban Missile Crisis. Moody was a SIGINT expert for the National Security Agency (NSA). She was responsible for gathering and analyzing enemy radio and electronic communications. In 1961, she was put in charge of studying communications between the Soviet Union and Cuba. A year later, when the Cuban Missile Crisis began, she was right in the middle of things. Moody made key decisions about which intercepted and decoded Russian messages to relay to her boss, NSA director Lieutenant General Gordon Blake, before he met with President Kennedy and his advisers. She stayed inside Washington, D.C.'s NSA offices throughout the crisis, taking short naps on a cot in her office. Several years afterward, she was recognized for her outstanding service during such a difficult time.

Perhaps the most controversial woman spy of the Cold War period was Elizabeth Bentley. Bentley began her spying career as a Soviet agent, then she switched sides and helped expose many Americans working undercover for the Soviets. The information that Bentley provided caused a big stir within the intelligence communities on both sides in the Cold War.

Born in Connecticut, Bentley studied in Italy during the 1930s, where she had a professor who was a communist. After

In the first half of the 20th century, communism appealed to workers who wanted their voices heard.

returning home, she joined the American Communist Party and then volunteered to become a spy for the group. She was assigned a handler who was in charge of a group of Russian spies, several of whom were American government employees. Bentley became the handler's girlfriend and then took on a key role maintaining communications between him and the agents. The Soviets gave her a code name that meant "Clever Girl." When her boyfriend died of a heart attack, Bentley expected to take over his group. Soviet intelligence leaders did not agree. Bentley became upset—and also began to worry that the Russians might try to eliminate her. So, in August 1945, she went to the FBI and offered to become an informant. In later meetings, she revealed more than 150 names of Russian spies working in the U.S., including 37 government employees. FBI director J. Edgar Hoover informed British intelligence chief Sir William Stephenson about Bentley, who in turn told high-ranking MI6 executive Kim Philby. That was a mistake because Philby was a Russian mole. He reported the events to Moscow, and spying activity of Bentley's group was shut down just as the FBI was beginning to follow the people she had identified. The result was that the U.S. government was unable to make a good case against any of the suspected spies.

Bentley was later called on to testify at several spy trials, including that of Julius

Even though Bentley swore to tell the truth to the U.S. Senate, doubt was cast on her testimony.

and Ethel Rosenberg. She was also questioned at Congressional hearings during the early 1950s about communists alleged to be working inside the U.S. government. Her testimony made headlines throughout the country. While some of what Bentley claimed was probably true, she also had a tendency to exaggerate, and her credibility was questioned. When she died of cancer in 1963, few people noticed. She was never given credit for the role she played in Cold War counterespionage efforts.

CHECKPOINT CHARLIE

Dozens of spy novels and movies about the Cold War have featured a key crossing point between West and East Berlin known as Checkpoint Charlie. The crossing, established after the Berlin Wall was erected in 1961, included a small guard hut, gates that could be lifted and lowered to regulate car and foot traffic, and two signs that read "You are leaving the American sector" on one side of the border and "You are entering the American sector" on the other. It is likely that hundreds of spies looked around cautiously as they passed through the checkpoint to get to or from East Berlin and that several spy exchanges took place there.

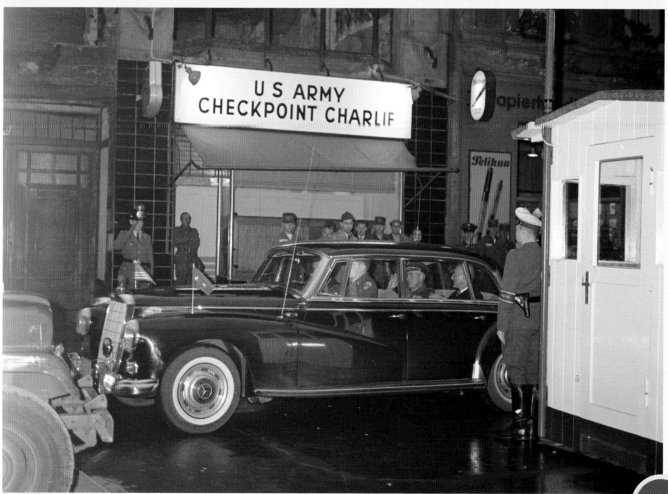

All vehicles were subject to inspection at Checkpoint Charlie during the Cold War.

The story of veteran CIA operative Jeanne Vertefeuille (*VER-tah-fay*) had a more positive ending than Bentley's. Vertefeuille joined the CIA as a typist in 1954 and quickly worked her way up the ranks. She was a quiet, private person who did her work very well but chose not to stand out. In some ways, it was a surprise when, in 1986, Vertefeuille was picked to lead a small task force of CIA employees looking into why several of the agency's Russian double agents had recently disappeared and were presumed dead. One possible explanation was that there might be a Russian mole inside the CIA exposing the double agents.

Vertefeuille set out to find the mole and thought she had the answer three years later while studying financial records of longtime CIA agent Aldrich Ames. Ames was in charge of counterintelligence in the CIA's Soviet division, so he often came in contact with KGB counterparts. Ames also seemed to be living far above his means. He drove expensive cars and had a home that seemed too costly for his government salary. Still, the investigation stalled.

Finally, in 1992, a deeper examination of Ames's records showed that he had made several large deposits in his bank account soon after meeting with Soviet officials as part of his job. The FBI was called in, and Ames was finally arrested in February 1994, eight years after Vertefeuille began her investigation. Vertefeuille was in the interrogation room when Ames was brought in for questioning. He gave her a sly look and said that he had tried to get the KGB to shift blame onto her as the real mole. "At first I wanted to jump across the table and strangle him," Vertefeuille said, "but then I started laughing. It was really funny, because he was the one in shackles, not me." Vertefeuille and fellow CIA agent Sandra Grimes wrote a book entitled *Circle of Treason* about the hunt for Ames. A television miniseries called *The Assets*, based on the book, was aired in 2014.

One of the suspicious things that led to Aldrich Ames's arrest was his purchase of a $50,000 Jaguar.

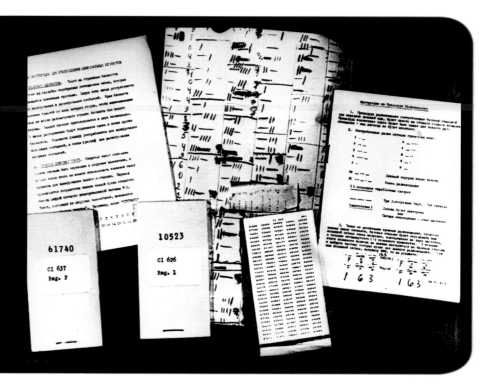

CHAPTER FOUR

SEEING DOUBLE

THERE ARE TWO SIDES to spying—espionage and counter-espionage. Espionage involves sending spies undercover to discover and transmit enemy secrets, persuading individuals in enemy territory to spy for your side, or conducting covert activities to undermine the enemy. Counterespionage involves identifying and capturing enemy agents or creating processes to prevent enemy spying in your country. During the Cold War, each side tried to advance both its espionage and counterespionage capabilities. There were some notable successes and a number of dismal failures.

The Soviets were successful in recruiting spies inside the U.S. and Great Britain during and after World War II, as was evident with their infiltration of the Manhattan Project and the enlisting of communist-leaning British students such as Kim Philby. But the U.S. had its own successful program to counter these spies. It was called the Venona Project and involved capturing and *decrypting* messages sent by Soviet Union intelligence groups. A team of American SIGINT specialists, both men and women, pored over Soviet documents throughout the Cold War period. Thanks largely to the work of Venona

Scrutiny of foreign mail couldn't catch all espionage—especially when spies were trained to use codebooks.

staffers, spies such as Klaus Fuchs, the Rosenbergs, and Philby and his Cambridge friends were identified and stopped.

Unfortunately, the Venona intercepts did not identify one troublesome double agent working for the Soviets inside MI6 in the 1950s. He would play a key role in undermining a major espionage project early in the Cold War. The setting was East Berlin, Germany. Following World War II, Germany and its former capital of Berlin had been divided into two sectors. The U.S., Britain, and France oversaw West Germany and West Berlin, while the Soviets controlled East Germany and East Berlin. In October 1953, a group of CIA and MI6 leaders came up with a plan to build a tunnel from West Berlin into East Berlin to be used to tap phone lines of Soviet military and intelligence leaders.

The tunnel took more than a year to dig and was supposed to be top secret. It wasn't. One of the MI6 agents at the original meeting to plan the tunnel was George Blake, who was actually a Soviet mole. He made sure the Russians knew about the tunnel all along. Still, they let it be built and even allowed the Americans and British to tap thousands of phone calls between May 1955 and April 1956 so that no one would suspect Blake as a double agent. Some of the calls contained real information, and others were full of disinformation that the Soviets hoped would

fool listeners. Then the Soviets "accidentally discovered" the tunnel while doing some maintenance work beneath their military headquarters and blocked it off. Blake, meanwhile, continued to work for the Soviets until 1961, when a Polish communist defector revealed his spying to MI6. Blake was tried and imprisoned but later escaped and fled to the Soviet Union.

Throughout the Cold War years, the CIA made it a top priority to recruit Soviet intelligence officers both to learn inside information about enemy activities and to help uncover spies working inside U.S. intelligence agencies. They had moderate success. Oleg Penkovsky was

Hidden tunnels did not remain hidden for long when both sides were on the lookout for spies.

A "COOL" HOTLINE

During the Cuban Missile Crisis, U.S. president John F. Kennedy and Soviet premier Nikita Khrushchev communicated with each other several times, issuing demands and responses. But the communications process was dangerously slow and tedious. After the crisis was resolved, both sides decided to install a special 24/7 "hotline" so that the White House and Kremlin could get in touch quickly in case of a political emergency. The hotline officially went into operation on August 30, 1963. It was not used until June 1967, when president Lyndon B. Johnson notified Soviet leader Alexei Kosygin that he was considering sending American planes into the Mediterranean during a war involving Israel, Egypt, and Syria.

The close communication enjoyed by Kosygin and Johnson in 1967 briefly improved international relations.

perhaps the best-known U.S. mole. Another was Dmitri Polyakov, who spied for the U.S. for more than 20 years. Thanks to Polyakov, the U.S. learned that the Soviet Union and China were at odds with each other. This knowledge helped U.S. president Richard Nixon decide to develop closer relations with China, starting in 1972. Polyakov also provided key details about Russian weapons that were being sold to other countries and might be used against the U.S. or its allies. Polyakov's CIA contacts were surprised when he suddenly stopped communicating with them in 1986. Later, they learned that Polyakov had been executed after being betrayed by American double agents Aldrich Ames and Robert Hanssen. Before they were finally caught and thrown in jail, Ames and Hanssen revealed many vital American secrets and betrayed numerous U.S. moles.

During the early 1960s, CIA leaders became obsessed with trying to overthrow Cuban dictator Fidel Castro and even to have him assassinated. There were two main reasons: the U.S. thought that Castro might help to spread communism into other countries in Latin America, and Americans didn't like how Castro's government had taken over American businesses that had thrived in Cuba before he assumed power in 1959. All the efforts to topple Castro were unsuccessful. One of the worst failures occurred on April 17, 1961, when a CIA-trained group of Cuban rebels living outside their country attempted an invasion at a place in southern Cuba called the Bay of Pigs. Unfortunately, Castro had been warned about the attack, and his forces quickly defeated the rebels and imprisoned more than 1,200. The U.S. government agreed to exchange millions of dollars' worth of food and medicine to Cuba for the release of most of the prisoners.

CIA leaders were still determined to eliminate Castro, and several wild assassination plots were drawn up. One involved having a local *asset* exchange a poisoned cigar for one of Castro's supply. The cigar was provided, but the asset backed out at the last minute. Another plan called for emptying a poison capsule into a milkshake to be served to Castro while he was dining at a hotel in the capital city of Havana. This one also fell apart when the waiter/assassin could not get the capsule

Castro's speeches against the U.S. and its policies often served to further antagonize the CIA.

unstuck from the hotel's freezer, and the poison spilled out. Castro once jokingly said about the attempts on his life, "If surviving assassination attempts were an Olympic event, I would win the gold medal."

The CIA was more successful in helping topple another communist-leaning Latin American leader, this time in Chile. In September 1973, CIA-backed military officers overthrew Chile's president Salvador Allende and replaced him with General Augusto Pinochet. The new leader was more supportive of American interests, but he proved to be ruthless toward his people and reportedly had thousands of protesters killed during his early years in power.

One incredible CIA success story from 1980 was the basis for the award-winning 2012 movie *Argo*. The movie was based on real events that took place several months after a mob of radical Iranian Muslims stormed the U.S. embassy in Tehran, the capital of Iran, and took 52 Americans hostage. Six embassy staff members who were not captured went into hiding in the homes of Canadian diplomats. The CIA knew where they were, and agency leaders began thinking up plans to get them out.

Tony Mendez, a CIA operative who specialized in inventing believable covers for American agents, devised a plan to free the hiding diplomats and bring them back home. Mendez posed as a Canadian movie producer and flew to Iran supposedly looking for good locations in Tehran to film a new sci-fi movie. He brought along fake papers that identified the embassy personnel as members of the film production team and attached their photos to the papers. For several days, Mendez prepped the diplomats on film production basics—in case they were asked questions by Iranian security personnel—and went carefully over the escape plans. Then they went as a group to the airport in Tehran and made their way through several security checkpoints. The real-life events were almost as dramatic as those shown in the movie. At last, the group boarded a plane and flew out of Iran. (The remaining hostages in Iran were released on January 20, 1981.) Full details about the escape were kept hidden in top-secret CIA files for almost 20 years and were not made publicly known until the late 1990s.

*After being bombed
in 1973, the Chilean
presidential palace
La Moneda was
restored by 1981.*

END *of an* ERA

UNLIKE MOST TRADITIONAL WARS, the Cold War did not end with one side surrendering to the other or signing a peace treaty. It came to an end because both sides were tired of threatening each other and living under threats. They were also tired of spending billions of dollars on weapons, defense systems, and spy operations. The excessive spending was causing the Soviet Union to go broke by the late 1980s. The country had spent so much on the space and arms races during the Cold War that it had ignored many of the economic needs of its people, and they were suffering. Communism was also losing its appeal to many people living behind the Iron

In the U.S., the later years of the Cold War coincided with a cultural movement marked by protests.

Curtain. In an effort to keep the Soviet Union together, premier Mikhail Gorbachev initiated two reform plans known as *glasnost* (openness) and *perestroika* (restructuring). To his surprise, the policies instead encouraged many republics aligned with Russia in the Soviet Union to declare their independence. By 1991, the Soviet Union no longer existed. Even the KGB was disbanded and replaced by two organizations called the SVR and FSB, whose missions were directed more toward dealing with industrial espionage (spying in business situations) than with military matters and national security.

The Cold War era had been costly to the U.S. as well, both in terms of money and domestic harmony. The country had participated in two bloody anti-communist wars in Korea and Vietnam, and many Americans felt less trust in their government's policies. They were more divided than ever in their opinions about how the country's military and intelligence systems should act. An era of unrest was ending, but another even more disturbing period was just beginning with the rise of aggressive terrorist organizations in several parts of the world. Many people wondered if the next big war would be a hot one.

COVERT OPS
SPEAKING AT THE WALL

The Berlin Wall was a harsh symbol of the Cold War. It was also the site of two important Cold War speeches by U.S. presidents. The Wall was erected in August 1961 as a way to keep East Germans from escaping to the West. On June 26, 1963, president John F. Kennedy, speaking not far from the Wall, declared in German, "I am a Berliner" and that all Berliners should be free to move about their city. President Ronald Reagan seemed to echo Kennedy's words when he stood in front of the Wall on June 12, 1987, and urged Russian leaders, "Tear down this wall!" The Wall was finally dismantled on November 9, 1989.

43

COLD WAR
TIMELINE

APRIL 24, 1945 — U.S. president Harry S. Truman is first briefed about the development of an atomic bomb by the U.S. military.

SEPTEMBER 18, 1947 — The Central Intelligence Agency (CIA) is officially formed to coordinate U.S. foreign spying operations.

FEBRUARY 9, 1950 — U.S. senator Joseph McCarthy announces that he has a list of communists who are working in the U.S. State Department.

MAY 1952 — During a sweep of the U.S. ambassador's office in Moscow, a listening device is discovered hidden inside a large wooden plaque.

JUNE 19, 1953 — Convicted spies Julius and Ethel Rosenberg are executed for their part in helping the Soviets obtain secrets about the atomic bomb.

OCTOBER 23– NOVEMBER 10, 1956 — Hungarians start a revolution against Soviet communist control of their country. The Soviet army crushes the revolt.

OCTOBER 4, 1957 — Soviets successfully launch *Sputnik I*, the world's first artificial satellite.

FEBRUARY 16, 1959 — Fidel Castro is sworn in as prime minister of Cuba. He will eventually install a communist government.

MAY 1, 1960 — An American U-2 spy plane is shot down while flying over the Soviet Union, and pilot Francis Gary Powers is captured.

APRIL 17, 1961 — Fidel Castro's forces quickly put down the CIA-directed invasion of Cuba at the Bay of Pigs.

AUGUST 13, 1961 — The Berlin Wall is erected in an effort to stop East German residents from escaping to the West.

OCTOBER 15-28, 1962	The Cuban Missile Crisis nearly brings about a nuclear weapons confrontation between the U.S. and Soviet Union.
JANUARY 23, 1963	Kim Philby, a high-ranking official in Great Britain's MI6, defects to the Soviet Union.
AUGUST 1965	The U.S. commits combat troops to South Vietnam as part of the war with communist North Vietnam.
AUGUST 1968	The Soviet army crushes an anti-communist uprising in Czechoslovakia.
JANUARY 28, 1980	CIA agent Tony Mendez helps six American embassy staff members escape from Iran in the "Canadian Caper" operation.
APRIL 1985	CIA agent Aldrich Ames volunteers to become a mole for the KGB. He is caught and arrested in February 1994 after a long investigation.
OCTOBER 1985	FBI agent Robert Hanssen begins spying for the Soviet Union. He is finally caught in February 2001 and sentenced to life in prison.
NOVEMBER 9, 1989	The Berlin Wall starts coming down, and plans are made to combine West Germany and East Germany into a single country again.
DECEMBER 8, 1991	The Soviet Union is officially abolished.

GLOSSARY

AGENTS—people who work for an intelligence service; spies

ASSET—a local person acting as a spy for a foreign agency or providing secret information to a spy

ASYLUM—protection given by a government to someone who has left another country in order to escape being arrested or harmed

CAPITALISM—an economic and political system in which a country's trade and industry are controlled by private owners (rather than the state) for profit

COMMUNISM—a political and economic system in which all goods and property are owned by the state and shared by all members of the public

COVERS—made-up occupations or purposes of agents

CRYPTANALYSTS—experts at translating secret messages into normal language

DEAD DROPS—secure locations that usually include a sealed container where spies and their handlers can exchange information or intelligence materials to avoid meeting in person

DECRYPTING—breaking a code and making a coded message understandable

DEFECTORS—people who desert their country or cause and join an opposing side

DEMOCRACY—a form of government in which people have the power to make decisions directly or have indirect power vested in elected representatives

DISINFORMATION—false or misleading intelligence, often provided by double agents or issued by an organization as propaganda

DOUBLE AGENTS—spies who pretend to work for one country or organization while acting on behalf of another

EMBASSY—the headquarters of an ambassador and staff in a foreign country

HANDLER—a person who trains or is responsible for spies working in a certain place

INFILTRATION—the process of secretly entering or joining a group or organization in order to get information or do harm

INTELLIGENCE—information of political or military value uncovered and transmitted by a spy

MOLES—employees of one intelligence service who actually work for another service or who work undercover within the enemy group in order to gather intelligence

RECONNAISSANCE—scouting or exploring, often for a militaristic or strategic purpose

TRADECRAFT—the procedures, techniques, and devices used by spies to do their work

SELECTED BIBLIOGRAPHY

Campbell, Geoffrey A. *The Home Front: The Cold War in the United States.* San Diego, Calif.: Lucent Books, 2003.

Coleman, Janet Wyman. *Secrets, Lies, Gizmos, and Spies: A History of Spies and Espionage.* New York: Abrams Books for Young Readers, 2006.

Fridell, Ron. *Spying: The Modern World of Espionage.* Brookfield, Conn.: Twenty-First Century Books, 2002.

Hunter, Ryan Ann. *In Disguise! Undercover with Real Women Spies.* Hillsboro, Ore.: Beyond Words, 2013.

Janeczko, Paul B. *The Dark Game: True Spy Stories.* Somerville, Mass.: Candlewick Press, 2010.

Keeley, Jennifer. *Espionage.* San Diego, Calif.: Lucent Books, 2003.

Platt, Richard. *Eyewitness: Spy.* New York: DK, 2009.

Sulick, Michael J. *Spying in America: Espionage from the Revolutionary War to the Dawn of the Cold War.* Washington, D.C.: Georgetown University Press, 2012.

WEBSITES

CIA MUSEUM COLLECTION
https://www.cia.gov/about-cia/cia-museum/experience-the-collection/index.html
Stories, biographies, and a detailed timeline of events during the Cold War years.

ROYAL AIR FORCE MUSEUM NATIONAL COLD WAR EXHIBITION
http://www.nationalcoldwarexhibition.org/
An overview of people, places, and events of importance during the Cold War.

47

INDEX